Dedication

FROM THE AUTHOR

To my children—
Katherine, William, Nathan, and Margaret

ᖇᕬ

FROM THE ARTIST

To Kevin Turner and Voice of the Martyrs.
Thank you for teaching me that the whys of this life are hidden in the sovereign hand of God.

Acknowledgments

I would like to thank Ron DiCianni for his unstinting support
and for the invitation to be involved in this project.
And I especially thank my wife, Susan, for reading and rereading the manuscript with her X-ray eye.

Michael Card

ᖇᕬ

My thanks to:
Michael Card for listening and lending his talent to this book.
Lane Dennis and Crossway. Once again you've hit the mark.
Grant and Warren for asking me "why?"
My wife, Pat, who helps me cope with *my* whys.
Cindy Kiple—your designs are inspired.
My best friend, the Lord Jesus Christ, who didn't turn away when I recently asked Him, "Why?" . . . again.

Ron DiCianni

Lyrics from Michael Card's songs were taken from:

Chorus of Faith by Michael Card and Phil Naish ©1994 Birdwing Music/Davaub
Music. All rights administered by EMI Christian Music Publishing. International
copyright secured. All rights reserved. Used by permission.

Could It Be by Michael Card ©1988 Birdwing Music/Mole End Music. All rights
administered by EMI Christian Music Publishing. International copyright
secured. All rights reserved. Used by permission.

Flesh of His Flesh by Michael Card ©1988 Birdwing Music/Mole End Music. All
rights administered by EMI Christian Music Publishing. International copyright
secured. All rights reserved. Used by permission.

In the Wilderness by Michael Card ©1989 Birdwing Music. All rights administered by EMI Christian Music Publishing. International copyright secured. All
rights reserved. Used by permission.

Jesus Let Us Come to Know You by Michael Card. ©1982 Mole End Music (admin.
by Word Music, Inc.). All rights reserved. Used by permission.

That's What Faith Must Be by Michael Card ©1988 Birdwing Music/Mole End
Music. All rights administered by EMI Christian Music Publishing. International
copyright secured. All rights reserved. Used by permission.

Why by Michael Card. ©1984 Mole End Music (admin. by Word Music, Inc.).
All rights reserved. Used by permission.

LIBRARY OF CONGRESS CATALOGING-IN-PUBLICATION DATA

Card, Michael, 1957–
    Tell me why : eternal answers to life's timeless questions /written by Michael Card : illustrations by Ron DiCianni.
        p.   cm.
    Summary: When an angel is sent to earth to discover a new song for the King, he meets a young boy with many questions and together they
begin to seek the answers.
    ISBN 1-58134-031-1 (hc. : alk. paper)
    [1. Angels Fiction. 2. Christian life Fiction.] I. DiCianni, Ron, ill.
II. Title.
PZ7.C1895Tg   1999
[Fic]—dc21
                                                99-21448
                                                CIP

15 14 13 12 11 10 09 08 07 06 05 04 03 02 01 00 99
15 14 13 12 11 10 9 8 7 6 5 4 3 2 1

Introduction

*I*f you could ask God one question, chances are it would not be a what, how, or when question, but a why question. Much about this road we call life has twists and turns that make us scratch our heads and wonder. But there is one thing more painful than the question itself. It's when the answer is silence.

The pages of the Bible are filled with stories of godly men and women asking why—Job, Moses, Elijah, Jeremiah, and even Jesus Himself while in human form. Even with the wonders of modern technology and all the advances society seems to have made through the years, the whys remain.

In God's divine plan He doesn't answer all our whys. Surely He could, but often He chooses not to. The reason is that He wants us to trust Him—in every situation. Yes, *every!* Isaiah said, "'For my thoughts are not your thoughts, neither are your ways my ways,'" declares the LORD. "'As the heavens are higher than the earth, so are my ways higher than your ways and my thoughts than your thoughts'" (55:8-9).

If you think this book is going to answer all your whys, keep your receipt handy. However, if talking through the *purposes* of the whys, which is what this book does, gives you some motivation to trust the one who knows all the answers, then read on.

James Dobson once said, "Never let yourself succumb to feelings of divine betrayal, which is Satan's most effective tool against us. Instead, store away your questions for a lengthy conversation on the other side, and then press on toward the mark." (Don't you have a feeling that "Why did You make mosquitoes?" will be in the top ten questions?)

In the final analysis, Hebrews 11:6 gives the definitive answer: "Without faith it is impossible to please God. . . ." It's not the statement we hope for, but it's the one we need to accept for now, so we can wait for that conversation when we see Him face to face. Take courage, friends—God knows the answer to every why, and knowing Him is better than knowing why. ❧

Michael and Ron

LISTENING FOR THE SONG

Theodas was only one of the thousands of angels who wrote new songs for the great King. For thousands of years he had labored at his task. He listened for new songs, writing sometimes first the words, then the music—sometimes the other way around. More often than not his songs pleased Christopher, the choir director. Then the angels in the choir of heaven would sing those songs in the Holy City. On those special times Theodas felt great joy. The angels played and sang his music perfectly. But above all, everyone in heaven who heard his music understood it perfectly.

One day an unheard of event happened. Theodas himself was called into the very presence of the great King. When first he heard the call echoing through the halls of the Holy City, he was filled with a thousand feelings all at once. He feared, he hoped, he longed, and he was overjoyed all at the same time.

Being an angel, he was used to light, but as he came near the great shining door of the throne room, even he was forced to look away. The thousands of bright beings around the throne slowly parted as he approached. They all seemed to know of the King's command that Theodas appear.

Covering his face with one of his great wings and his feet with the other wing, he bowed low before the throne. He waited in silence for the King to speak.

"Beloved one," the Voice like many waters said, "you have served me so long and so well. I desire" (for the great King is full of desire) "you to go down to the earth and listen for a new song" (for the great King loves hearing new songs). "Listen for a song unlike any you have ever written. It is my wish that you move about the face of the earth listening for a new song."

At first Theodas was filled with dread. He did not like the thought of leaving this bright place and going to that fallen and troubled world. In the same moment he was filled with joy at the thought of obeying the Great One and writing a new song that might praise and honor Him.

"I am the Lord's servant," he whispered behind his wing, still bowed low.

"Go then. Keep your eyes and ears open for one who will go with you, one who will understand without knowing what perfect praise is."

There was no further word, not even the least hint of any kind of send-off or good-bye. Theodas had only the sudden feeling of being surrounded by darkness, of breathing it in, of being weighed down by it.

He knew at once he had been sent to the earth. The very heaviness of the place brought a tear, his first, to his eye.

What would be for you and me a beautiful morning, for the angel was dim and gray, barely bright enough to see the scene around him. The colors of the flowers and trees, which for you and me would be dazzling, he could barely tell apart. It seemed a gray, flat, colorless world to him after heaven. He stood beside a dirt road in the middle of a broad plain with a low range of mountains far ahead.

The only thing that reminded the angel of heaven was hearing, every now and then, the song of a bird. It wasn't so much the notes of the song that made him think of the music of heaven, but the joyful obedience he could hear behind the bird's singing. For someone like Theodas, it wasn't the rightness of the notes but rather the heart behind the music that mattered most.

"Perhaps it won't be so bad here," he sighed to himself.

During his first few steps he felt as if lead weighed down his feet, for he was used to flying. But he soon caught on to how to walk through the thick air and the heavy gravity.

William awoke to the same glorious morning. He looked out the window at the sun sparkling through the trees. He wondered to himself, *What makes the sun shine?* You see William was of an age where the whole world was to him one big "why."

Fortunately, from his mother he had learned never to fear questions, indeed never to fear anything but the great King. She taught him this rare courage not only with the words of her mouth, but also by the fearless life she lived out before her son.

From his father William learned how to say the words, "I don't know." Now that may not sound important, but indeed besides knowing you know a thing, it is just as important, and even more so, to realize when you don't know a thing. This takes altogether another kind of special courage. His father, who was the greatest of men in William's eyes, was always ready to say when he didn't know something. But in the same breath William's father was always just as eager to say, "Let's go and find out."

The boy sprang from his bed, ready for whatever the day had in store for him. Little could he realize now just how much that would be!

William set out excited with all the sights and sounds and smells of the morning. As he wet his feet with the dew of the grass, he wondered, *Where does dew come from?* As he heard the birds singing overhead, he called up to them, "Who taught you to sing that song?" (Like Theodas, William especially loved to hear the birds sing.) As he drank in the smell of the garden, he wondered, *How is it flowers smell so sweet?* You see, William wondered at the world, and as he did so, the world became wonderful for him.

The thought of all that could happen during an entire day was almost more than his imagination could bear. The freedom, the promise of so many good things to see and do made the young boy dizzy.

He sat down in the grass, paying no attention to the dew, and quietly waited to hear the bird sing once more. All at once a shadow came over the place where he was sitting. It was an older boy from the village. The boy's name was Wendell.

"What you think you're doing?" Wendell spoke with meanness in his voice. Just as William began to answer, Wendell hurled a stone in the direction of the branches, striking the songbird squarely on its multicolored chest. The beautiful bird fell lifeless at William's feet.

"That will teach you to sing, huh!" Wendell hissed.

William's morning was ruined. He fought back the urge both to punch Wendell and to cry out at the bird's cruel death.

The bully towered over the young boy, his hands on his hips. "You're the stupidest boy in the village. You will never amount to anything!"

This, of course, made William even angrier. He buried his head in his arms and hugged his knees, trying to keep himself from either bursting into tears or bursting into Wendell with his fists.

"What is this?" A strong, calm voice spoke from behind them.

The two boys turned to see the tall figure of a man standing in the cool shade of a nearby tree. He had been silently watching them. He kept his distance, not wanting them to see that his own face was wet with tears.

"Nothing!" the bully blurted back. "Besides, it's none of your business!"

"How could one so young possibly know what my business is or isn't," the man said, straining to still sound kind. "Be off with you, little snake, and may your heart be broken someday the way you have broken a heart this day."

Wendell had never been spoken to in such a strange and mysterious way. He simply did not know what to say. There was nothing left for him to do but turn and slink away.

William was wiping the tears from his face as the tall figure made his way over to him. The man too towered over the boy, but not in a frightening way as Wendell had. The stranger seemed to be there to protect William.

The man looked down and wiped a few tears from his own face. "Who are you?" he asked.

"William," came the quiet reply, because for now for William his name was all he was.

"Come, sit with me over here," the angel said, pointing. Taking William's hand, he led the boy away from the lifeless, songless bird, away from his pain and anger and over to the shade of the tree.

They sat together silently, both wondering how the world could be so beautiful and yet so cruel.

"Thank you." William finally smiled after a long time.

"You are most welcome," came the gentle reply.

"Who are you?" William asked. "I've never seen you in the village before."

"I am a stranger in this strange land of yours." Theodas did not simply answer with his name, because he knew that our names aren't all we are. And besides, angels sometimes like to keep their names a secret.

"Do you have a place to stay?" William asked with a leftover hiccup.

"No," the angel said. "I've only just arrived."

"I'm sure my parents would welcome you to our house—that is, if you have no place else to go."

"That would please me," Theodas said with a smile.

Hand in hand, they set off for the boy's house.

❦

The two found William's father at work at his potter's wheel. They stood silently watching the careful movements of the potter's feet, as he spun the wheel, and his hands, as he smoothed and shaped the wet, gray clay.

So caught up was William's father in his work that he didn't notice the two for a long time. Finally, as he took a break to wipe the sweat from his brow, he saw his son and the tall stranger.

"Good morning," he said, as always with welcoming joy and kindness.

Theodas shaded his eyes with one of his great hands and looked to see the position of the sun. "The morning's almost gone," he said with as much warmth as William's father.

"This is a stranger who has no place to stay. Might he stay with us?" William asked.

"He cannot stay," his father said with an uncharacteristic wrinkle on his brow. "That is—as long as he is a stranger. But new friends are always welcome under our roof."

William's father had a way of saying things that drew people in. William had expected a yes in answer to his question. But as usual his father answered in an interesting and unexpected way.

"After all, 'Some have taken in angels without knowing it,'" the potter said with a smile. Of course, he was saying more than he knew. And for now Theodas determined that no one need know the truth of *what* he was.

The angel was shown a tiny corner room directly above William's. There was only a plain bed barely long enough for him, with a thin mattress, and a simple chair and table. What made the room special was not the house but the *home* it was in. Though Theodas was used to the far more beautiful rooms and furniture of heaven, he settled in soon enough.

As father and son came down the stairs together, William began to tell what Wendell had done to the songbird. They made their way back to the potter's shed, and William felt his face getting hot once more just at the pain of telling it.

As usual his father did not answer right away. He knew that one of the best ways to show people that you love them is to listen to them. William was well loved by both his parents in this way. The potter sat at his wheel and started it spinning once again with a strong kick. The pot he was working on before being interrupted had "melted" into a heap, and so he was forced to start all over again.

He scraped the mass of clay into a lump. Holding it close to him, he began to pound the lump with his fist to force out any trapped air. William had, of course, seen him do this before, but it was not until this moment that he wondered why. The questioning look on his face let his father know what was on his mind.

"Oh, I'm pounding out the air. You see, if there are any pockets of air in the pots, they will burst when they are put in the fire to be baked."

Having finished this important step, William's father placed the lump of clay back onto the center.

"What about Wendell, Father? Why is he so cruel? Why does he treat people the way he does?" With each question William's voice grew louder.

"You were really hurt by him, weren't you, my son?" his father said, seeing his pain.

"Why, yes. He ruined my day. He killed that beautiful bird for no reason. He made me so angry!"

"Perhaps Wendell has not yet given his life to the great King, as you have. And also has it occurred to you that if it had not happened just so, perhaps your new friend would never have found you or a place to stay for the night?"

"I don't know if Wendell even believes there is a great King. But still, why did it have to hurt? Couldn't the stranger just as easily have found me by the sound of my laughter?"

"I don't know, my son." The potter looked at the lump of clay that was slowly becoming a useful pot. "Remember how I pounded the clay to make it ready to be shaped? Perhaps that's part of what all our hurts are about. The great King knows that there are 'pockets' within us that must be pounded free before He can begin to shape us and make us ready for the fiery tests of life. Sometimes the pounding hurts. William, I cannot tell you any more than this because I don't understand any more than this, but I *believe* there is a purpose in the pain. And I trust the great King. And never forget that even the Son of the great King learned through the things that hurt Him."

"I'm not sure I understand," the boy said, looking not at his father but at the clay spinning on the wheel.

"I'm not sure I *understand* either, my son. But I am sure that I *believe*."

In a shadow in the corner at the foot of the stairs, a tall, silent figure stood listening to their discussion as if it were some sort of beautiful song.

"What a wonderful melody!" Theodas whispered to himself. He knew then that he had come to the right place.

In the wilderness
In the wilderness
He calls His sons and daughters
To the wilderness.
But He gives grace sufficient
To survive any test,
And that's the painful purpose
Of the wilderness.

MICHAEL CARD
from "In the Wilderness"

Why do I need faith?

HEAR WHAT THE SILENCE SAYS

A short distance down the street lived an elderly couple. They were related to William in some sort of way that his mother was never able to make perfectly clear to him. And so he simply called them "Aunt" and "Uncle." Not only were William's relatives old, but his uncle was blind, and his aunt was deaf. This always made visiting them an interesting adventure for William.

When his mother discovered that the visitor staying with them was hungry, she realized there was not enough food for the evening meal. So William and Theodas were sent to his aunt and uncle's house to borrow some flour and a few vegetables for a simple supper.

It was just beginning to get dark out as they came to the small house. William knew he had to knock loudly on the door in order to be heard.

"Is anyone home?" William asked even though he knew there was *always* someone home.

The person who opened the door was small and gray and stooped over. The old man leaned on the doorknob and squinted with blind eyes into the darkness outside.

"Who is there?" a soft and gentle voice asked.

"It's me—William."

"Sweet William!" the old man said with a sound of delight in his voice. He reached out and found William's hand. "Why, come in, my boy."

Though he could not see that there was someone else with William, his uncle sensed somehow that Theodas was there. You see, people who have lost the use of their eyes often learn to "see" in other ways.

"Who has come along with you?" the old man asked.

"This is a new friend, a stranger to our town, who is staying in our house tonight."

"You are most welcome in our home," a woman's voice said almost in a whisper from somewhere in the back of the room.

It was William's aunt. Standing beside a rough wooden table, she was just beginning to prepare their own supper. She too was short, like her husband. In fact, Theodas was amazed at how much the old couple looked alike. Since he was an angel, and no one in heaven ever marries, Theodas did not know that people who are married a long time begin to look like each other. These are the kinds of wonderful things earthbound people know that angels don't!

The old woman's eyes were intelligent and bright. Her smile was real and welcoming. Though she was deaf, she had seen William and the tall stranger come in and greet her husband. She understood by the smiles on their faces exactly what was happening. You see, people who have lost the use of their ears often learn other ways to "hear" what is going on around them.

"Come in and make yourself at home," the old man said, standing between the two visitors. His hands were on their shoulders guiding them in, and he was being guided at the same time by them.

Theodas looked around at the bare room. When he had first seen how simple and empty William's house was, he was surprised. He wondered if everyone on the earth lived in such poor places. After all, he was used to the riches of heaven. His feet were accustomed to walking on glistening golden streets. His eyes had seen sights too beautiful for words. But now in a strange sort of way, he began to see the poor, simple house of William's relatives as somehow beautiful in its own earthly way.

"William, it's good to see you," his blind uncle said.

"But you can't see me, Uncle, can you?" the boy asked.

"I see you perfectly in my mind and in my heart, my boy. Your face is as familiar to me as that of anyone I know."

Theodas smiled to himself as he listened to their conversation. Having always lived in heaven, he had never seen anyone who was blind or deaf. He had only heard about such things when people in heaven talked about all that the Son of the great King would do away with when He returned to earth.

"You are welcome to stay and eat with us," William's aunt said. Because of her deafness she had never heard the sound of her own voice, and so she spoke in her own special way. William liked to hear her speak.

His uncle made some signs with his hands that explained to her that they had only come to borrow some flour and vegetables for their own supper. The old lady nodded and smiled, leaving the room by the back door and heading out to the garden for fresh vegetables.

"Is it hard for you to talk to your wife?" Theodas spoke for the first time.

Turning his head in the direction of the angel's voice, the old man laughed, as if the question was some kind of joke.

"Why, of course not," he said. I have loved that woman now for fifty years. Deaf or not, I love talking to her. She is the best listener I have ever met."

William giggled, trying to understand what his uncle could possibly be talking about.

"What!" said the old man, turning toward the boy. "Don't you believe me? William, someday you will learn that you use more than your ears to listen, even as I use more than my eyes to see. Eyes go blind. Ears go deaf. But the desire of the great King is that we should always listen, that we should always try to see."

The words of William's uncle sounded like the lyrics of a great heavenly song to Theodas.

"Uncle, I see how you talk on your fingers to Aunt and that she understands. I think I know what you mean when you say that you can see my face inside your heart in spite of your blindness. But I still don't understand how this can be. What makes these wonderful things possible?"

"Certainly you have heard of 'faith'?" Theodas spoke up. "You must have faith to see what is unseen and to hear what the silence says. Where I come from everyone understands these things."

Just then William's aunt came in with more than enough vegetables for their supper under one arm and with a large container of flour under the other.

"I hope these will be enough," she said in her unusual but gentle voice. Everyone smiled at her generosity.

Both William and Theodas were quiet as they made their way home. The angel was wondering at the kindly old couple. The openness and warmth with which he, a stranger, was received was as beautiful to him as anything he had ever seen in heaven.

William was thinking about how it could be possible for someone to see without using his eyes or hear without using his ears. He was trying to remember what his uncle had said about faith making this wonderful miracle possible.

"What do you think my uncle meant when he talked about faith? Why do we need faith?" The boy stopped and looked up at the angel.

"You believe in the great King and His only Son, don't you?"

"Why, yes," William said.

"Have you ever seen His face before or heard His voice?"

"No."

"And yet you still say that you believe?"

"Yes."

"That is faith."

Theodas glanced up at the starry sky as if he were looking for help in finding just the right words. "We need faith so we can see," he said with a musical tone in his voice, almost as if he were about to begin singing the answer. "Without it all of us are blind. We need faith so we can see and hope so that we will want to see."

The two made their way home in the dark, but to William it would never seem quite as dark again.

To hear with my heart, to see with my soul;
To be guided by a hand I cannot hold.
To trust in a way that I cannot see—
That's what faith must be.

MICHAEL CARD
from "That's What Faith Must Be"

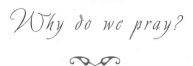

HAVING THE ANSWER

ot too far away from William's home lived one of his closest friends. Her name was Susan, and she, though three years older than he, was smaller than William. This is because she was born with what people called a "weak heart."

William never completely understood this. He thought Susan had a strong heart, a brave and beautiful heart. And it was precisely because of this that he liked her so much.

If ever his father was busy in the potter's shed or his mother too busy about the house, Susan was always the first person to whom William would go with one of the "why" questions for which he was so well known.

On this gray morning William had no particular question on his mind. He only wanted Susan to meet his mysterious new friend. When the two arrived at her house and knocked softly, Susan's mother came to the door with a worried look on her face. You could see that she had been crying. Her face was puffy, and her eyes were red.

"William!" she said with gladness. "I know Susan will want to see you."

"Is anything the matter?" William asked anxiously.

"She has been terribly weak for the last three days. She doesn't even feel like eating. I'm so worried. Talk to her. She'll listen to you."

As William and Theodas walked past Susan's mother, she looked up into the angel's face and smiled. His heart was warmed that in spite of her worry and concern for her sick daughter, she still could find it in herself to give a smile to a stranger.

The little girl was lying on her bed in a small room just off the main part of the house. Against one wall was a doll's table and chair with some toy cups for tea parties. Beside her bed was a small pile of books. They looked well worn, as if she spent a lot of time in bed reading.

"Will," she said in a whisper. She seemed really glad to see her friend.

"Susan, what's wrong?" William had seen her ill before, but she had never looked as bad as this.

"I don't know what it is," she said. "I just feel tired all the time."

"Your mother says you won't eat. You must eat, Susan, so you will feel better." The tone of

William's voice spoke all the worry he had in his heart for his good friend.

"Who is your friend?" she asked, brushing aside his urging.

"He's a stranger who has just come to our town, but he is my friend."

Theodas bent over the girl's bed and looked down smiling. "We are sorry you're not well, little one," he said with as much compassion as William. He took her small, cold hand in his big, warm hand. When he said "we," it seemed as if he meant someone else besides himself and William. In fact he did, for Theodas spoke for the great King as well.

The angel was silent for a time. In his imagination he saw the struggle going on in the heavenlies for the cause of the young girl. He could see battle lines forming on either side as a fight for her life began.

"What if we prayed for her?" William asked, looking up into Theodas's face.

"Exactly what I was thinking," the angel responded.

Taking Susan's other hand in his, William closed his eyes tightly and began to pray, "Oh, great King, my friend is sick. She is tired too. Won't You come and put Your hand on her so she will get better?"

Theodas had never heard William pray before. He was pleased that the boy spoke so simply to the King, without trying to impress Him with big words. The angel, who knew the great King well, was sure that the prayer had been heard. In his imagination he saw that those fighting for Susan on the side of the great King were strengthened by William's prayer. Even at that moment an answer was being given.

As the boy quietly prayed, the young girl fell asleep.

"We should go now," Theodas said, motioning to the door. He knew that all that could be done had been done.

With that, the two got up from the bedside and tiptoed out of the room.

"Thank you for coming," Susan's mother said. She felt better now that someone besides herself knew about Susan's illness and had prayed for her. "Please come back tomorrow."

As the two made their way home, William asked the angel, "Why do we pray anyhow? Doesn't the great King already know what we need?"

"Yes," the angel said.

"Doesn't He care about Susan as much as I do?"

"Yes, a great deal more, I should say."

"Doesn't He want her well as much as I do?"

"Yes."

"Then why would He want us to pray when He knows all along what He is going to do?"

"Fathers want to hear the voices of their children, I suppose," Theodas said. William remembered a time when his own father had said exactly the same thing.

"The things that their children need, their hurts, their problems, their questions—all these things bring children to their fathers. Without the needs and the hurts many children would never come. But fathers love being needed and sometimes wait for their children to come and ask, even when they already know what the children will ask for."

"And the great King is like that?" the boy asked, scratching his head. Though he believed in the great King, he had never thought of Him as a father.

"Something like that," the angel said looking down at William with a kind smile.

Early the next morning William went alone to see how Susan was feeling. Just as he was coming to her house, he saw the doctor leaving. There was a worried look on the man's face.

The door was left open, and so he peeked in. There he saw Susan's mother kneeling beside her daughter's bed. The pale little girl was lying there very still.

"She is getting worse. I feel so helpless. Please help my daughter." Her mother was whispering and praying and crying all at the same time.

William had slipped quietly and respectfully into the room. He stood by the door for a long time, looking at his friend on the bed and feeling pretty helpless himself. All at once he sensed a Presence in the room. It felt like his father's presence, but it wasn't his father. It felt like Theodas's presence, but the angel was still at home. It was the Presence of the great King.

Susan's mother continued to pray, but in a way unlike he had ever heard anyone pray before. She spoke as if the life of her daughter depended on her prayer. William began to wonder if it did.

"I don't know what else to say," she pleaded. "Only You can save my daughter now. She belongs to You, O King. Please heal her!"

Susan's mother slowly got up from her knees. As she turned, she saw William, but she was too tired to be surprised.

William stood there, still feeling the Presence of the great King. He spoke almost without realizing it. "I believe she will get better. The battle is won. Don't be afraid."

Without answering, Susan's mother smiled a weary smile and walked out the door. It was a tired but not a hopeless smile.

Susan got much, much worse before finally, after a time, she began to improve. William did not understand this. But from that time on, he always knew he was being heard when he prayed. And even when he wasn't praying, when he was laughing or simply being sadly quiet, he knew the Presence was there still, listening. When he tried to explain all this to Theodas, the angel only smiled a knowing smile.

"Remember when you asked me, 'Why do we pray?'" he reminded. "Do you understand now?"

"I'm not sure," William sighed. "I remember what you said about the battle and our needs and hurts and how the King is like a father who longs to hear our voices. But when I prayed for Susan, He didn't answer for a long time. All that happened was that I felt his Presence. It is as if the great King some-times only gives Himself as an answer."

"Is having Him as good as getting an answer?" the angel asked.

"I think maybe having Him *is* the answer," William said, with a grown-up tone in his voice that he had never had before.

Theodas looked the boy in the face and smiled. The angel felt more tears coming to his eyes.

"More tears," he laughed. And just at that moment he heard far in the back of his head the faintest beginning of what sounded like a song.

In our words and in our silence,
In our pride and in our shame,
To the genius and the scholar,
To the foolish and insane,
To the ones who care to seek You,
To the ones who never will,
You are the only answer even still.

Could it be You make Your presence known
So often by Your absence?
Could it be that questions tell us more
Than answers ever do?
Could it be that You would really rather die
Than live without us?
Could it be the only answer that means anything
is You?

MICHAEL CARD
from "Could It Be?"

BARELY ROOM TO STAND

It was early Sunday morning. It had now been three days since Theodas had come to stay at William's house. He seemed interested neither in going nor in staying. At whatever moment, in whatever place he was, he always seemed completely satisfied.

As time went on, William began to wonder more and more just who this tall, quiet stranger really was. For one thing, he wasn't sure exactly where Theodas went early every morning. Was he meeting with someone on some sort of business? Did he just want to be alone? And so one morning the boy decided to follow him.

The angel made his way out of town toward a part of the country everyone called the "wasteland." There were no farms or homes here. The land was too barren to raise even sheep, which could get by on next to nothing.

William could just barely make out Theodas's tall figure against the early morning sky. The boy walked slowly behind his strange, silent friend, keeping a distance so as not to be discovered.

What William could not have known was that Theodas knew from the first moment that he was being followed and by whom. But somehow he didn't mind. In fact, he welcomed the young boy on this particular morning, for on this morning he was to report on the progress of his mission. He was going to pray as he always did, but also he was to meet with Christopher, the chief musician of heaven.

Theodas arrived at the lonely place where he was used to praying and knelt down on the hard, dry earth. William stayed some distance away, believing himself to be hidden behind a bush. As the angel went to prayer, a stillness came over the place. It was the same stillness William had experienced in Susan's room—the Presence of the King.

"My deepest thanks for another day," Theodas began in earnest, "and for the chance to follow and to serve You, O King."

Just then William's nose began to itch. His eyes began to water, and he could feel a sneeze coming on. He tried to stop it, and soon the urge disappeared. Then all at once the sneeze came bursting out, surprising both William and Theodas, who jumped ever so slightly.

"William?" he said softly without looking around.

"Sir?" the boy answered, not knowing what to say. (He had never called Theodas "sir" before.)

"You followed me. Why?"

"I was wondering where you were going so early in the morning." William began to step from behind the bush as he spoke.

"Now that you know, would you like to stay and pray with me?"

"Why, yes." The boy was surprised that Theodas did not scold him for his sneaking around. Instead he was invited to share this most special of all times.

"You asked me once who I am. I told you I am a stranger. Have you never wanted to know more?" Theodas asked.

"Yes, I suppose that's why I'm here."

"Come then and kneel beside me," the angel said in a way that was mysterious and yet kind. (If you ever want to really know who someone is, pray with the person.)

William found kneeling on the bare ground painful. In a very few minutes his knees began to ache. But then something happened that made him forget his knees. As the two knelt in prayer, a golden light began to glow in front of them. There was a fragrance in the air like a thousand flowers. William tried to keep his head bowed, as he knew he was supposed to do, but what was happening before him was too wonderful to shut out.

In the midst of the ever-growing light, he could make out the form of a man—at least he thought it was a man. Theodas glanced sideways to see if William was watching. There was an eager smile on the angel's face.

As the figure drew near, William began to hear a sound unlike any he had ever heard before. The only word he could use to describe it was *music*, but this was more than music. Sure enough, it was a sound, he thought, but it was a sound that went through him, that almost came from inside of him. He felt as if he could have stopped up his ears and still heard it perfectly well.

The figure moved out of the light and stood before them. He was taller even than Theodas. He looked down at the two, with his hands on his hips, an ordinary thing to do, William thought, for such an extraordinary being. It was a long time before the newcomer spoke. "And what of your mission, Theodas?" Christopher asked the still-kneeling angel. "Have you heard the song you were sent to hear?"

"Theodas? Is that your name?" William whispered. He suddenly realized that he had never thought to ask his name.

"Well enough, by the grace of the great King," came the solemn answer. "I hear new notes every day."

"And who is the young man?" Christopher asked, glancing toward the place where William was still kneeling.

"This is William, my friend." Theodas spoke without looking either up at Christopher or toward William. "He belongs to the great King and so has shown great kindness to me from the moment I arrived. His family opened their home to me, not knowing what I am."

"*What* you are?" William whispered to himself, yet still loud enough for the two angels to hear.

"I will tell the King when I return that they are worthy of great honor," Theodas said, now looking up.

"You are missed in the Holy City, Theodas. We long for your return. Continue in your mission and do not be surprised if you begin to experience some changes in your body. These changes will be the result of your stay on the earth. You may begin to feel more tired after a time. After all, you are a being who was created for eternity, and time will soon change you the way it does every man. But do not worry—the Great One, of course, understands all this from His own stay here on earth. He will not leave you nor forsake you."

With these final words the shining figure turned back toward the golden light, stepping into it the way you or I might enter a room. As he moved away, the light grew dimmer and the mysterious music faded, but the fragrance was still in the air like a memory.

"Why are you looking at me that way?" the angel asked with a smile. "Don't be afraid."

"But I am afraid," William whispered. "Why didn't you tell me?"

"You never asked."

"It's not exactly the kind of question you ask someone. 'How are you?' 'How's the weather?' 'Are you an all-powerful angel from heaven?'" William smiled as he realized what he had just said.

"Not 'all-powerful.' Only the great King is that. I am only a servant, like you. My power comes from His command."

"You can fly?"

"Well, not here, it seems," Theodas said, looking back at the place where his great wings used to be.

"Why are you here?"

"I am a musician of the great King. He sent me to listen for a new song. He loves hearing new songs."

The two stood up and had begun to make their way back in the direction of home when suddenly William realized what day it was.

"Sunday!" he gasped. "It is church day, and if I don't hurry, my father will be looking for me."

The two began to hurry, William taking two steps for each great stride of his friend.

"What is it like to be an angel? How long will you stay? Could you teach me to fly before you go?" William, now feeling more himself, started thinking of questions again.

"There are some things I am not allowed to tell you, William. And others you would not be able to understand," Theodas laughed as he stood up to the barrage of questions.

"Why not? After all, we're alone. Who would hear?"

"Alone—." Theodas stopped in his tracks and looked straight at William. "We are never alone, William. Perhaps that is one thing I can tell you. I know it has been done before."

"What has been done before?" William asked with a note of fear. Suddenly he was sorry for asking all the questions when it seemed he might face the possibility of actually having one of them answered. Besides, he was still in a hurry to get to church and find his father.

"I know there have been times, long ago, when the eyes of people have been opened so they could see that they are never alone." Theodas sounded as solemn as when he had spoken to Christopher.

"But we are alone! Just look. It's only you and me. Come on, let's go!" William's hand swept outward in a large circle.

"If you could only see the truth, young one, there is barely room for us to stand. We are surrounded." Theodas spoke with a breathless tone. He looked around them as if his eyes were meeting the glances of a thousand faces.

"I don't believe you!" William said.

"Would you like to see?" Theodas asked as if certain William would refuse.

"See *what*?"

"The multitude of people and angels. The witnesses. They are like a cloud about us."

With that Theodas reached out his hand to William. "Take my hand and close your eyes."

Though it was shaking with fear, William stretched out his hand to the angel, who took it in his own warm hand.

"Now close your eyes and tell me what you see."

William shut his eyes. "Nothing," he said with the same disbelieving tone in his voice.

Theodas squeezed his hand tighter and whispered a prayer that the great King would open William's blind eyes. All at once, though his eyes were closed, William saw a brilliant flash. It was like lightning lighting up a dark landscape. And in the instant of that flash he saw what must have been millions of bright beings standing all around them as far as he could see. The hillsides were covered with them. They were crowded all around, close enough to touch. The sight took his breath away. As quickly as it had come, the light left. He let go of the angel's hand and stepped back in amazement.

"And now what do you say?" Theodas asked.

"There are no words for it," William gasped, out of breath. "It's just as you say; there is barely room for us to stand. They are all around us."

"Never forget this, William. You will never be alone because you can never be alone. The air is full of angels."

The two walked on, William still speechless from his experience. Soon they came to the simple wooden building where William and his family went to church. They slipped in just as the sermon was beginning. William's father, as if sensing his son had come in, turned and smiled at seeing both of them sitting on the back row.

The pastor of the church was a kind man who usually spoke softly. He was one of William's favorite people for answering questions. The pastor stood behind the pulpit, simply dressed. He was not making a grand speech, but talking as someone who loved his people and was telling them the truth. But how was William supposed to listen after such an experience as the one he had just had on the road with the angel? And so he sat there trying to remember the scene that the lightning flash had lit up in his mind when he took Theodas's hand.

Just then a thought struck him. Perhaps in this, of all places, there might also be many witnesses crowding all around. And so with tingling fingers, he reached out and took Theodas's hand once more. The angel smiled, knowing instantly what the boy was doing.

Once more William closed his eyes and held on tightly to the angel's hand. And once more the scene all around him changed; only this time it was not with a flash as much as a warm glow. In the glow of the light William saw all around their pastor a group of shining men and women. Some of them he recognized from books, famous Christians who had gone to heaven long ago. Others he had never seen. They were listening right along with the people in the pews. Some of the heavenly beings were nodding in agreement, others often bowing their heads in prayer for the pastor. Once again the scene took William's breath away.

After the service, as they slowly walked home, William was quiet and thoughtful.

"Friend, you have seen and experienced much today," Theodas said as they walked along.

"The world will never be the same for me," William replied. "Going to this church will never be the same. To think that all these people pack themselves into that small building to be with us, to watch and encourage and listen. I used to ask Father why we go to church. He told me we went to learn to follow God. Now I have another reason. People who have already gone to heaven and the angels are there cheering me on."

"You're right, William," agreed Theodas. "And your friends and the grownups at church are also there to help you, and you are there to help them as you do God's work together."

"I never understood that following the great King meant I was a part of something this wonderful. It's a miracle!"

"You would be surprised at how quickly people forget miracles," the angel said, looking down and kicking up a cloud of dust.

"I was wondering, Theodas, how do you handle seeing those wonderful shining beings all the time? Is it ever too much for you?"

"That's funny," the angel said. "I was just wondering how you could handle life *without* seeing them."

We are flesh of His flesh,
Bone of His bone.
His Spirit has brought us
Together as one.
Though we may be separate,
We're one perfect whole,
For we are His body,
And He is our soul.

We are the blessed receivers
Of His inexhaustible love,
And so it is out of believers
The body of Christ is made of.

Forever we'll have one another
Because we belong to the Lord,
And so we belong to each other,
And that is our greatest reward.

We are flesh of His flesh,
Bone of His bone.
His Spirit has brought us
Together as one.
Though we may be separate,
We're one perfect whole,
For we are His body,
And He is our soul.

MICHAEL CARD
from "Flesh of His Flesh"

THE SONG IS YOUR LIFE

*N*ow that William had discovered just *what* Theodas was, you can only imagine how many questions came tearing through his mind. The angel had made it clear that he wanted William to keep his secret. They made sure no one else was around when they talked about it.

"What is heaven like?" William whispered one rainy day.

"It is beyond words, my friend, in many ways. That's why when people here are given a glimpse of heaven, they come back with descriptions of pearly gates and golden streets. The truth is, it is more beautiful even than that. And still in other, more important ways, it is much like the earth. There is a wonderful stillness there at times, like your mornings here. There are acts of kindness and smiles and great moments of laughter. There are green fields like some I have seen here. Oh yes, and music. They are forever singing there, sometimes along with you down here. There is not enough singing here, it seems to me!"

Sometimes Theodas would speak about heavenly things without being asked. Once after the two had seen a fight between two men in the town, the angel began to talk about some of the battles he had fought in.

"Michael, you know, is the archangel who is the leader of the heavenly army whenever we go into battle." He spoke without looking at William. There was a far-off look on his face as he remembered a battle on some distant hillside.

"He is mighty for the King, but in moments away from the fight, he can also be the most gentle of beings. I saw him weep openly once like a child. That was when the Son of the great King died on the cross. The King had ordered Michael to stand still, which was, of course, the last thing he wanted to do. He wanted to go protect the Son whom he, like the entire army, dearly loves.

"When finally the Son gave the victory shout from the cross, which sounded to Michael almost like the battle cry itself, I saw the great warrior angel hide his face behind one of his great wings and cry like a baby. The sight was too much both for what was strong and for what was tender in him."

"When you go into battle, what is it like?" William asked, wide-eyed.

"It is wonderful and terrible all at once. There are the shrieks of the dark ones, against whom we struggle. Now that is a horrible sound. To hear those pitiful, wretched beings, who know from the very start that the battle must be ours, to hear them wail as they return to the dark depths—it makes your blood run cold."

"But you said it can be wonderful too."

"Oh yes, most wonderful. Often mixed in with those awful sounds are the victory shouts of our army and sometimes even their laughter. The army of heaven cannot be beaten."

"Because you are all so strong?"

"Why, of course not. We cannot lose because the Son won the victory so long ago. On that cross He destroyed the power of the Evil One forever. That is when and where the war was won. There are only these troublesome battles left to fight."

"So you must still fight?"

"What you mean is, *we* must fight."

William did not have a clue as to what Theodas meant. "I've never fought in a battle," he said.

"Nothing could be further from the truth, my friend. Every day you are fighting, and I am fighting along right beside you—God's army and I."

"When?"

"When Wendell bullied you. When you prayed for Susan. When you wanted to take that ball that wasn't yours and didn't. When you were tempted to say something unkind to your father. When—"

"Those are battles?"

"Of course. Sometimes great battles. And as you fight on here, there is a struggle going on in heaven. You see, we *are* fighting together. We are both warriors, you and I."

"Is that why the cloud of witnesses you let me see is there?"

"That is one reason."

"You know, now that I hear you say it, it does feel like a battle sometimes," William said with a slow nod.

"Yes, and don't you sometimes feel as if you've been wounded?"

"Why, sometimes I do!" The boy exclaimed, his voice rising.

"And often the wounds are deep. Some of them take a long time to heal. Indeed some will never heal until the Son comes with healing in His wings."

"Is that why I am here? To fight?"

"No, you were not created for this. Neither was the great multitude of heavenly beings nor I. But we must, nonetheless, fight on until He returns."

"Then what was I created for?"

"To sing, of course," the angel answered, as if the question had been, "Is the sky blue?" or "Is the sun hot?" "To sing in the Garden along with those in heaven and with the King. People were made for the Garden. Have you never heard?"

"I had begun to wonder if that story was really true."

"Nothing is truer, you can be sure. Oh, what a glorious garden it was! Created just as a place for you to walk with the great King, to share your deepest thoughts and feelings with Him, to sing and laugh with Him there. A place where He offered His friendship, and yet people did not want it! How could you?"

Theodas frowned at William as if William himself were responsible.

"What do you mean? I—"

"I'm sorry. I know you weren't the first one to say no to Him. But still you do say no—you and all people. And that is what keeps you out of the Garden of His Presence."

"Hasn't anyone said yes?"

"Why, of course. The Son of the great King answered yes for you all. And so He invites you back into the Garden, back into a friendship with His Father, which only He had before."

"Friendship?" William gasped in amazement at the thought of being friends with God.

"Friendship," the angel answered with a beaming smile. "That is the greatest desire of the heart of the great King. That is what the Garden was for, what the Temple was for—places for His people to come and be close to Him. That was the reward for keeping His law (which no one but the Son was able to do). He wants to walk with you, William. You were made for eternity, William—not time. You were created to sing in the Presence of the great King. And so you shall when the time comes."

All these ideas were too much for William to take in at one time. He would need a lifetime. So, for the moment, he stopped thinking about them and, with a note of sadness in his voice, said, "I'm afraid I'm not very good at singing." He looked down at the ground.

Theodas seemed puzzled. You see, singing for a citizen of heaven means much more than the sounds you make with your lips. He had never heard William try to sing notes with his voice, but that didn't make the least difference to him. Singing, for the angel, was something you could do without making a sound. Songs, for him, could be moments of kindness or understanding or forgiveness. In fact he heard a person's entire life as a kind of song. That is what he had come to listen to and for, and so he was truly puzzled by what William had said.

"Not very good? Why, your singing is some of the most beautiful I've heard since I've been here. How can you speak such nonsense? Your song is the one I was sent here to listen to and take back to sing for the great King. You can be sure that He loves to hear you singing it."

"But I *never* sing! Everyone makes fun of me when I do. Even my father's eyes squint when I try!"

"William, the song is not the sounds you make to music. The song is your *life*. You are the poem, the song, and the masterpiece! The beauty of the song comes from the great King who created you and me."

Sometimes when we hear, not just any words but the perfect words, something moves inside us. And for William these were the perfect words. A curtain lifted inside, and for the first time he began to see, not what he was trying to do or be, but what in fact the great King had already done. The beauty he was beginning to see in himself was not anything he could ever be proud of, because it was not his beauty but the King's.

"A song you say?" He looked at Theodas as the rain outside began to stop falling and the sun broke through.

"A song," he said with a warm smile. "Don't ever be afraid to sing it nor to rejoice in the singing of it, for this is what you were created to do. You were made to rejoice with the great King, His Son, and the Presence for all eternity."

"Okay," William said with a frustrated laugh, trying to take it all in. It was hard to accept the marvelous words he was hearing because deep inside he knew that Theodas knew he couldn't carry a tune in a bucket.

Sing it with your life, sing with your heart,
Make melody with the words of your mouth,
But mind that you listen, tell it to others,
Hear the chorus of faith,
Live the chorus of faith.

The first note of the song split the darkness
And was sung by the planets and stars,
And their light spoke "hallelujah,"
And the words of the chorus
Were sung by angels before us.
Now come join in the tune.

MICHAEL CARD
from "Chorus of Faith"

THE FINAL VERSE OF THE SONG

Hours turned into days and days into weeks until no one could remember exactly how long Theodas had been staying at the house. By now William's parents had begun to suspect *what* Theodas might be, but they kept this to themselves and wondered if perhaps the angel had been sent to their son for a purpose that was beyond them for the moment.

By the end of the third week the changes Christopher had warned Theodas about began to show in his body. Though he had first come in the form of perhaps a twenty-year-old, he rapidly grew older through what would have been his forties if indeed he had been a person rather than an angel.

On this morning of his twenty-second day, you would have thought him to be in his seventies. His hair had gone from gray to white. His great stride had shortened considerably so that William could now easily keep up with him on their long daily walks. But even though Theodas seemed to be getting old fast, his mind remained razor-sharp, his heart ever tender and true.

"Where would you like to go this morning?" William asked as they sat across from each other at breakfast.

"Have you ever been to the top of the mountain?" William's father asked as he headed out the door to the potter's shed.

"No," Theodas replied through a mouthful of bread. "We have saved that trip for today."

"The mountaintop it is then," William said, clapping his hands and rubbing them together.

William's mother packed them a lunch as usual.

The morning was bright, but there was a wet feel of rain in the air. To the west they could barely make out a line of gray that could later in the day become a rainstorm.

Fall was in the air as well that morning. Many of the leaves had already turned golden or brown. William did not like fall. He would always say he was more of a "spring person." Spring was a season much more full of "whys" than fall. He did not like the colors of fall. He did not like the shorter days. He most especially did not like things dying all around him. Theodas knew this about William and could read across his face this morning that he was feeling a bit sad.

"Fall means the cycle of the seasons is almost complete, doesn't it?" he asked his silent companion.

"It means that everything is going to die," William said sadly without looking up.

"Like the songbird Wendell killed?"

"It seems like the whole world is falling apart to me."

"Kind of like me," Theodas said as he limped along. This morning he looked small and gray, like William's uncle. Though they had yet to reach the uphill part of the path, Theodas was out of breath already.

"Are you all right?" William asked. His love for the angel brought him out of his gloomy mood.

"I will be perfectly all right very soon," Theodas replied.

With that, the two walked on for a time, Theodas humming over and over to himself a simple tune.

"What is that?" William asked at length about the tune.

"It is almost finished," the angel said with great satisfaction in his voice.

"A song?"

"A new song."

William remembered what Theodas had said about his mission, about coming to the earth to listen for a new song for the great King. He asked, "The song you were sent to hear and write—is it finished?"

"Almost. It needs only one final verse."

There was something more behind what Theodas said, but William was unable to find the words to ask him. They continued toward the mountain in silence.

As they started up the steep slope, the angel stumbled, scraping his shin. He was out of breath and in pain.

"We could go back if you want," William said.

Without answering, Theodas went on, leaving William all the more worried.

Halfway up the mountain Theodas looked as if he were about to faint.

"Please, let's go back now," William pleaded.

"Good friend, I must make this climb."

"What if you can't make it? What if—"

"What if I die?" Theodas looked William in the face.

The boy felt panic at hearing those words. "Is that what you've come here for? To die?"

Theodas did not answer the question because he could tell by the sound of William's voice that the boy knew the answer well enough.

"Let's push on. Here, let me lean on you."

As the two climbed slowly up the mountain, the sky that had been threatening in the morning now became gray in earnest. The wind began to pick up as well, as they came nearer the top.

Within sight of the mountaintop, Theodas was forced to stop and rest one last time. "Please, just a moment here," he asked in a pitiful voice.

William, who had been struggling to think of the right words, blurted out, "Why? Why should an angel die?"

"I was created for eternity, not time, William, just like you. What has happened to me in the past weeks will happen to you as well as the years go on. It's like the falling of the leaves."

"But why don't you just return the way you came? Can't Christopher just send someone for you?"

"It's the song, William. I must hear the final verse if I am to write it for my King."

"The song?"

"It's why I came. To listen for the song, the beautiful song of your life and mine together. The song of our friendship, our fellowship, all that we've seen together, laughed and cried about. It will be a wonderful song. But there remains one final . . ."

"Then let me die instead!" William shouted, meaning completely what he said.

"No, that's not how it goes. This thing is for me to do. But I want you to stay here with me."

They sat silently together for a few more minutes until Theodas got up one more time to try to make it to the top of the mountain. At last they took the final step and stood on the summit. They collapsed together, waiting for the threatening sky to let go.

Theodas leaned back against a tree twisted by the constant wind on the top of the mountain. He looked old and somehow twisted by time as well. He gazed at what little view the dark clouds did not hide. He was pale.

"Yes, I hear it now," he said with a grateful smile.

"What is it like?" William, always so full of questions, asked.

"It is major and minor at the same time, darkness and light. This will be the most difficult part to write, I'm afraid," Theodas said with a mischievous cough.

"This does not have to end this way," the boy said, partly out of desperation and partly out of anger.

"This is not an ending, good friend. Are you still so dull?" Theodas reached out a weak fist and tapped William's forehead with a smile. "Remember the witnesses? Remember closing your eyes so you could see with your faith? Remember praying and having your prayer answered? This is merely the final pounding of the clay. That is all."

As he spoke these words, the rain suddenly began to come down in sheets all around them, wetting Theodas's white hair and wrinkled face. At the same instant William thought he could smell the faintest scent of flowers, though he knew very well that it was fall and there were no flowers about to smell.

He rested Theodas's head on his lap, sensing either that he had died or that he was close to dying.

"I've never known anyone like you," he said, choking back the tears. "You've always helped me find the answers I need."

Behind him a faint light was beginning to glow. It became brighter and brighter, pushing back the clouds and the rain by its very brightness. But William could not see the light for the darkness he was feeling in his own heart. It was finally the aroma like that of a thousand flowers that aroused him. He turned to see Christopher stepping out of the light. Beside him was Someone else William did not recognize. This person was tall, and, unexpectedly, His hands were wounded.

"William," the Great One said in a gentle voice, "I have come for Theodas. His work is finished now."

He bent down, taking Theodas's cold, dead hand out of William's. The boy could clearly see a scar just above His wrist.

"Come, my dear, dear friend," He said in the tone of a father and a brother and a friend. There was not even a hint of sadness in His voice.

At first William did not notice, but with the touch of the Great One's hand, Theodas's face was no longer pale, his hair no longer gray. And with a fierce gasp, he came to life again.

"But—you—were—"

"Dead—go ahead, say it," Theodas urged smiling. His young voice was back.

"What was it like?" William, always himself, couldn't resist asking.

"It was like being asleep and waking up again."

"But how could—"

"William," the tall wounded Man said, "there will be another time for having all your questions answered. Now is the time for us to return to My Father."

"Then you are—"

"The Son," He said.

At the sound of those words Christopher, Theodas, and William all bowed low. Though William knew nothing of the rules of heaven, it seemed to him upon hearing those words that there was nothing else to do.

When, after a few seconds, he looked up again, everyone else was gone. The rain had stopped. The smell of flowers still lingered in the air. And he thought he could hear the faintest notes of a song in the wind.

William fell back into the wet grass and laughed out loud to the clearing sky.

Jesus, let us

Come to know You,

Let us see You

Face to face.

Touch us, hold us,

Use us, mold us,

Only let us

Live in You.

Jesus, draw us

Ever nearer.

Hold us in Your

Loving arms.

Wrap us in Your

Gentle presence,

And when the end comes,

Bring us home.

MICHAEL CARD
From "Jesus, Let Us Come to Know You"

A BROTHER TO THE SON
OF THE GREAT KING

*T*heodas had once said that it is surprising how quickly people forget about miracles, and he was right. After a few weeks William's life settled back to what it had been before. To be sure, it was a different life. He still felt the Presence from time to time. He had the vision of the cloud of witnesses still firmly in place in his youthful memory. He, of course, knew much more than he had before Theodas had come.

But he quickly discovered that knowing things with your mind doesn't always make a difference in the way you live. He still fought battles with fear and with anger. He was still wounded in these struggles from time to time, but they were, for the most part, wounds that healed quickly.

In time, however, William began to feel the weariness that comes from trying to fight battles all alone. Yes, he knew about the witnesses. You see, though he knew about them in his head and that he was himself the King's warrior, he forgot it in his heart. He found himself "stretching the truth" a bit at times when he was in trouble with his parents. More and more often he got into squabbles with his friends and sometimes was surprised at how selfish he could be. Once he even cheated on a test.

One day, when he was at his lowest, William decided it was too hard to keep doing the right thing. He was going to give up fighting. It seemed to him it would be so much easier to follow in the footsteps of people who did what they liked when they liked without thinking of anyone but themselves—like Wendell.

"It's not worth it anymore," he said as he spied a knife he wanted on a table in the marketplace. He had wanted that knife for a long time but had never had the money to buy it. He had asked his father for the money, knowing all along that his father couldn't afford it either.

He found himself making his way to his uncle's house. Knocking on the door, he heard no reply.

"Since this is market day, they will go into town to buy food," he said, as finally a truly criminal thought made its way into his heart. It was a thought completely wrong for one who was supposed to be in the service of the great King. "I know where they hide their savings," he said to himself. "It will be a long time before they miss the money. Maybe I can even sneak back in later and replace it."

But even as he thought about replacing the money, he knew he had no intention of ever doing so. He was sickened at the falseness in his own heart.

William pushed open the door quietly. He was right—no one was at home. He found the tin box behind the fireplace where the elderly couple hid all their savings. He opened the box. He smelled the musty odor inside of old paper money. He took it out and counted enough for the knife, which left only a couple of dollars.

"I might as well take it all," he said, sticking the small wad of bills into his pocket.

As he made his way into town, he saw his aunt leading his uncle through the marketplace. He waited until they were safely out of sight before he went to the place where the knife still lay gleaming on the table.

"That one," he said, pointing to the peddler.

As he stood by the table counting out the money, he felt a frail hand on his shoulder.

"Sweet William, I heard your voice. Is that you?"

It was his uncle!

"Where have you been?" the old man asked.

"Uh, nowhere! What do you mean by that?" William stammered in a guilt-ridden voice.

"Nothing, only that we have missed seeing you."

What a stupid thing for an old blind man to say—"We have missed seeing you." Why does he always talk such nonsense? William thought to himself. And as he gave himself to that dark thought, he sensed that he had just committed a sin greater even than stealing the money. In a way that would be almost impossible to describe, he had just murdered the old man in his heart.

"I have to go," he blurted out. "My mother needs me." He was caught in a trap made out of lies. He knew his mother didn't even know where he was.

"My, you're in an awful hurry. Well, come and see us soon." His uncle, it seemed, belonged to another world, a world William had left behind the moment he decided to take the money.

William spun away from his uncle's grasp, not looking where he was going. In his panic to escape, he bumped his aunt, who had just come up behind them. He never stopped to help her pick up the groceries she dropped to the sidewalk. Seeing who it was, she called out in a pitiful voice, "William, it's me."

"But it's not me," he shouted back to her deaf ears.

William did not know where to run. Home was the last place he could go now. He did not want to see his mother. He knew exactly what she would ask as he came in the door—"Where have you been?" And he, in his guilt, would either explode with the truth or else tell yet another lie. He couldn't face either possibility now.

He could not go see his father at the potter's shed. What if his father was pounding a lump of clay? William knew that he himself would feel every blow of his father's fists. And Susan, with her tender heart, would know without asking that something terrible had happened. What could he possibly say to her?

There was nothing left for him but to run. So run he did, out of town and past the wasteland where once he had knelt with an angel and prayed, up the slope of the mountain. He hoped he would exhaust himself with the climb. He hoped even against hope that he might find in his exhaustion the "sleep" that Theodas had once found on the mountain.

As he reached the top, his heart was pounding in his ears, as much from his guilt as from the physical strain of the climb. He had run as far as his legs could carry him, and yet he had not gotten away from the guilt, from the pain, from the Presence that even now was weighing him down like lead.

"Here!" he screamed as he took the shiny new knife from his pocket and flung it off the cliff. "I never really wanted it anyway!"

He fell on his knees. It was the exact spot where Theodas had died, where William had held his hand, where he had seen the Son.

"I can't fight anymore! It's just—too hard."

Against hope, he strained to hear Theodas's familiar voice behind him. He sniffed the air for the smell of flowers. He squinted, thinking he might see a tinge of golden light. But all was silent except for the distant song of a bird. The only smell in the air was the earthy smell of the dust he was kneeling on. The only light was the ordinary light of day all around him. William, after all, had seen his share of miracles, and that is what he needed now, desperately needed. But no miracle came—only the miracle that there was no miracle.

He stayed at that spot for what seemed hours. His knees never felt the cruel ground until, his emotions exhausted, he finally tried to get up. He dusted himself off and turned to go home.

William had not heard him come up from behind. The boy turned to see his father standing there, worried and exhausted himself.

"I saw you running. I was worried, afraid something had happened to you."

William stumbled toward his father and collapsed in his arms. "Something *has* happened. I've lost my way, Father. I'm not me anymore. I'm not your son. I'm a thief, a liar, a murderer."

You might have thought that with each confession, William would have felt more guilt, but the exact opposite was true. Each confession was like a weight coming off.

"I know everything, my son," his father said, stroking his head. "I spoke to your uncle. He told me the money was missing. The peddler told me you had bought the knife. I didn't put two and two together until your aunt made the signs that told me you had knocked her down. What have you done, William?"

His father didn't expect to hear an answer. He was asking the question for himself and perhaps even asking for the sake of the great King.

"I just couldn't fight anymore," William said with an empty look on his face. "I'm tired of fighting by myself. It's too hard. It's too much to ask anyone."

As he fell back into complaining again, William sensed the burden coming back. It was as if chains were being placed on his hands and feet.

"You were never supposed to fight the battles by yourself, my son. I am here. Your mother is as well. But more important, the Son of the great King has promised He will never leave us. Remember, Theodas told you He has already won the battle for us."

"I had forgotten—No, I wanted to forget."

William could not get the image of the scarred hand out of his mind. That is what he wanted to forget. He had seen the miracles. He had walked with an angel. He had spent his life asking questions: "*How* is this possible?" "*Where* did it come from?" "*When* will it happen?" "*What* is it all about?" Never had he asked the most important question, the only true question: "Who?"

"Who is the Son, Father? I know He is the Son of the great King. I know He died on the cross. I know there are scars on His hands. I have seen them. But who is He?"

"Have you forgotten, my son? You must never forget that He died on the tree *for you*. It is not enough to know about the scars; you must remember they are *for you*.. Though you tried to let go of Him and run away from Him today, He never let go of you. You, my son, are a warrior of the great King. Get up; rejoin the battle along with me. Never forget you do not fight alone. William, you never stopped being my son today, and you never stopped being a son of the great King."

His father was right. William never ceased to be his father's son that day, and indeed he would never fight alone again. After all, he was a warrior of the Great One, a brother to the Son of the King. On that day all he knew about the Son became the music of his life.

Theodas returned to heaven with the song he had been sent to hear, the song of William's life. He wrote the words first and then the music. Christopher accepted the music and passed it on to the great choir, and Theodas had the joy of hearing it perfectly played and perfectly sung as it echoed in the halls of the Holy City. The great King, who is full of desire and loves hearing new songs, rejoiced in the tune as well as in Theodas's joyful obedience in writing the song.

A distant echo of the song fell on Wendell's ears just as he was about to crush some innocent victim, and his heart was broken by it. He turned from his life of cruelty and embraced the way of the Son of the great King.

Susan too heard an echo of the song and was strengthened by it, though her health remained a struggle all her life.

And finally William heard it one clear morning as he was trying to remember what the great crowd of heavenly beings he had seen on the hillsides looked like. By this time he had pretty much surrendered his "whys" for the great "Who" that had become the theme of the song of his life.

Why did it have to be a friend
who chose to betray the Lord?
And why did he use a kiss to show them
That's not what a kiss is for?

Only a friend can betray a friend.
A stranger has nothing to gain,
And only a friend comes close enough
To ever cause so much pain.

And why did there have to be a thorny crown
Pressed upon His head?
It should have been a royal one
Made of jewels and gold instead.

It had to be a crown of thorns
Because in this life that we live,
For all who would seek to love,
A thorn is all the world has to give.

And why did it have to be a heavy cross
He was made to bear?
And why did they nail His feet and hands?
His love would have held Him there.

It was a cross, for on a cross
A thief was supposed to pay.
And Jesus had come into the world
To steal every heart away.
Yes, Jesus had come into the world
To steal every heart away.

MICHAEL CARD
From "Why"

45

THE CLAY (page 5)

Each time an artist, sculptor, or other creative person begins a project, he or she envisions the end result before even lifting a brush or lump of clay. One time Michelangelo lingered before a rough block of marble so long that his companion asked him what he was doing. The great sculptor replied enthusiastically, "There's an angel in that block, and I'm going to liberate him!"

Well, inside of what we see in the mirror is a sculpture fit to stand in the museum of heaven. God is not going to be content until He finishes the job. He knows what we are supposed to look like.

God told Jeremiah, "Go down to the potter's house, and there I will give you my message." So Jeremiah obeyed. As he watched the potter at work, the pot became marred in the potter's hands. The potter then took the clay and made it into another pot. God's message came to Jeremiah: "O house of Israel, can I not do with you as this potter does?"

Outwardly the woman in this painting seems to have no need of additional shaping. However, the Master can look deep inside and see the cracks forming that will eventually undo her, if not repaired. As G. H. Knight remarked, "Nothing is more certain than that we will be perfectly satisfied with His work when we see it finished. Why should we not be satisfied now when He tells us what a glorious finish He will make, and leave to Him the choosing of the tools?"

NOAH (page 10)

Noah heard the voice of God telling him to build a boat. Keep in mind that it had never rained on the earth yet and that the boat would require some time to build—120 years' worth of time, amid the sneering and jeering of those around him. Did Noah get weary? Did he doubt? Did he feel like abandoning the project after, say, 95 years? The Bible doesn't say, but I know I sure would have.

When I ponder the massive scale of that project, my puny trials take on a new perspective. If Noah could work 120 years on a boat, maybe it's not such a big deal to work a year to develop a project for the church. If Noah could stand the jeers, maybe I can keep from buckling under the taunts of those who think I'm politically incorrect and insensitive to new "lifestyles." I might even be able to hang in there when God speaks in that still, small voice, asking for something I'm not quite sure is logical.

No matter what Noah did or didn't experience during that 120-year boat- and character-building project, imagine what he must have felt when the first raindrop fell. That is the moment to keep in mind when we get weary and are tempted to give up.

A MOTHER'S LOVE (page 14-15)

Here is a painting born out of my own experience. I remember as a young man walking past my parents' room and hearing my mom praying for me. I'm not sure how much that experience impacted me at the time. But I have come to realize now that it was pivotal. My mom's care to cover me with prayer and give God the right to do whatever it took to keep me reserved for Him set a pattern for me as a dad.

I hope this painting will be an encouragement to moms who choose to stay home with their kids. I didn't have a lot of things when I was growing up, but my mom was there when I came through the door. I don't miss the things.

Here a mother is praying at an unscheduled moment. Perhaps as she is going about picking up toys or cleaning, something reminds her of a need to pray, a moment of communion with her heavenly Father that somehow puts the rest of life in focus. Her daughter peeks in for a glimpse of security. Notice the cross being formed through the areas between the picture frames and observe the spiritual warfare in the upper left corner.

THE LEGACY (page 20-21)

People doing ministry long to follow in the footsteps of the Master to fulfill the same mission He did. They know they have been sent, not just to a job but to a calling. It doesn't take long, however, for many to realize the size of the shoes they are filling, as well as the difficulty of the task. Discouragement, doubt, and meager results sometimes tempt a servant to quit.

Is there a secret to survival? I believe there is. It may be found in remembering Who has commanded you. It is also found in realizing that you are not called to be successful—just obedient.

The express purpose of this painting is to encourage people in ministry that a "great cloud of witnesses" surrounds them (Hebrews 12:1). While John had to face those wanting to behead him for his preaching and Moses had the grumblers, ministers today contend with those watching the clock so as not to be late for the restaurant. While not as deadly, it's just as discouraging.

If each time a sermon is given, a minister could peek behind the curtain of time, he would see those who are cheering him on. And he can always claim Jesus' promise to be with us wherever two or three are gathered together. It's too early to quit. Jesus, John, Moses, Paul, Peter, Elisha, and many others are counting on us.

FELLOWSHIP (page 28-29)

God is our example. If He didn't think it a waste of time to walk with Enoch, then I have to believe it's not a waste of time for us to walk with our kids—or take them fishing, picnicking, or any other activity. I heard one family refer to it as "making memories." I like that.

Some time ago I read of a famous man who told of the one day of his life that meant the most to him. It was the day his father took a day off just to take him fishing. That day was a turning point in the son's life. Years passed, and the father died. Knowing that his dad had kept a journal, the son couldn't wait to see what his father had written of the day that had so impacted his life. When he turned to the page, he read:

"Spent the day fishing with my son. A day wasted."

Can you imagine the shock and disappointment of that moment?

Making the most of even those moments that don't appear to accomplish anything may be achieving more than we can ever know. One thing for sure—God approves. That's what this painting is all about.

SAFELY HOME (page 34)

This century has produced more martyrs for Christ than in all the previous centuries combined (119 million and counting). *Safely Home* is the victorious side of martyrdom. The long-awaited embrace from the greatest Martyr of all is more than enough reward for the saint who followed in His footsteps.

This scene is waiting to be reenacted for every believer who will someday stand before the King of kings and Lord of lords. While not many of us will be privileged to go out in a blaze of glory, Christ will still be waiting with open arms for all of His children.

You will notice that the martyr has received his crown. That's what we will lay at Christ's feet. The red runner points to the crown of thorns that He wore for us. An angel waits with a white garment to replace the tattered clothes of earth. Now that the chains are off, the martyr is free to dress for eternity. The floor is a map of the world, as Christ is ever conscious of where His children are suffering.

HE HOLDS THE KEYS (page 40)

"Don't fear: I am the First, I am the Last, I'm Alive. I died, but I came to life, and my life is now forever. See these keys in my hand? They open and lock Death's doors; they open and lock Hell's gates" (Rev. 1:18 THE MESSAGE).

Often we seriously underestimate the power and control of Jesus. If He has a firm grip on the keys to eternal doors, I'm not going to doubt that He has enough power to handle anything else. I constantly have to remind myself of G. K. Chesterton's comment to a woman who told him that God is not to be bothered with "small stuff." Chesterton replied, "Lady, to God it's all small stuff."

As I painted, I tried to imagine the scene in Ephesians 4:10 where Christ descended to open the gates of Hell, entered the dark dungeon that was the domain of His defeated foe, and released the captives. Holding the keys, Christ "ascended on high, [and] led captives in [his] train" (Ps. 68:18). I visualized the hope and anticipation of those hearing His footsteps coming to release them from bondage as they realize that never again will they suffer at the hands of the Evil One.

For more information on Ron DiCianni's work, please call 1-800-391-1136 or visit us online at www.art2see.com.